Prayer Scriptures for Prayer Warriors

For our struggle is not against enemies of blood and flesh, but against the rulers, against the authorities, against the cosmic powers of this present darkness, against the spiritual forces of evil in the heavenly places. — Ephesians 6:12

Energion Publications

ΣFastTracts

a gateway to spiritual growth

#5

Guidelines for Prayers

Pray each prayer for each person or group on your list.

Use the scripture prayers in addition to, not instead of your personal prayers to God.

Include praise and thanks in all your prayers.

While praying scriptural prayers mention specific people, events or groups.

Use your name or see a loved one in these scriptural prayers.

Pray for your church, prayer group, pastor, study group, family and friends with each of these prayers.

Find others to pray with you and for you.

Leave time to listen to what God has to say to you.

Remember that prayer is not a method. These are ideas to help you become more comfortable communing with God. I certainly hope you will develop many others.

For Truth and Blessing

Father, I thank You for *_____'s faith in the Lord Jesus and his love for all the saints. I will not stop giving thanks for him and praying for him. I ask in the name of Jesus, glorious Father, that You give him a spirit of wisdom and of revelation and a deep knowledge of You.

I pray that the eyes of his understanding be filled with light so he will know the hope of his calling, the richness of his glorious inheritance among the saints. I pray that he may know just how immeasurably great Your power is for those who have faith. I pray, Father, that he will recognize how effectively Your power works, just the way it did when You raised Christ from the dead.

I praise You, Father, that Jesus now sits at Your right hand in heavenly places, Father, above every power and authority and force of power and lordship and everyone's fame that can be mentioned not only in this world but in the world to come. All things have been subjected under the feet of Jesus, and He has become the head of his body, the church in all matters. He fills the universe everywhere!

— adapted from Ephesians 1:15-23

*fill in a name from your prayer list for each blank line or italicized pronoun.

That Each will Stand Firm

With the powerful grace of God in mind I kneel before You, Father. You are the One from Whom every family in heaven and on the earth gets its name. All fame belongs to You. I ask, Father, that You give _____ the power to reach into the inner man by the Spirit. I ask that Christ will dwell in his understanding through faith. I ask that with all the saints he be rooted deeply and grounded firmly in love, and be able to grasp just how wide and long and high and deep Your love is. May he know it, even though it is too great to really understand, so he may be filled with Your fullness.

Father, I give You the glory. May You receive praise from generation to generation forever, because You are the One Who works among us so powerfully that You are able to do more than we can ask or even imagine.

— adapted from Ephesians 3:14-21

For God's Armor

Father, I ask that _____'s strength come from being in Your mighty grasp. I ask that he be equipped with all Your armor, God, so that he can stand firm against the devil's schemes. I know, Lord, that we are not fighting against people, but rather against authorities, rulers in the darkness of this world, and against highly placed evil spiritual forces. So I pray that he put on all the armor that You provide. Then he will be able to stand firm when that evil day comes. I pray that he be able to stand all the way through the battle.

May he Stand ready!

Belt of Truth

Wrap truth around his waist as a belt

Breastplate of Righteousness

Let God's righteousness fully protect his torso as a breastplate

Shoes of Peace

May he be prepared with God's good news of peace

Shield of Faith

May he take up faith as a shield

Helmet of Salvation

Wrap God's salvation around his head like a helmet

Sword of the Spirit

And let him take up God's word as a sword.

Father, I lift up before You now prayers and petitions continually in the Spirit. [This is a good time to listen and pray as you feel led. All prayer should be prayer in the Spirit!] I intercede for _____ and petition You for him. I pray that he may have the right message to speak when he opens his mouth, to make known boldly the mystery of the gospel, even in chains. Let him be as bold as he ought to.

— adapted from Ephesians 6:10-20

For Protection

Lord, I live in Your hiding place, and I stay under Your shelter. Lord, You are my fortress and my refuge. I place my trust in You.

Lord, I ask that You keep me safe from hidden traps and deadly diseases. Spread Your wings over me so that I can find security. May your truth and faithfulness be my shield and defense.

I praise You Lord, that I don't need to worry about night terrors, nor about arrows flying during the day. I don't have to fear plagues striking in the darkness or sudden disaster at noon. Even though a thousand fall at my right side, or even ten thousand, I will be completely safe. I will see their destruction, but I won't be touched by it.

That's because You, Lord, are my place of refuge. You, Lord Most High are my fortress. No disaster will strike me anywhere, nor will I be wounded at home.

Father God, command your angels to guard me wherever I go. Let them grab me and lift me to safety if I stumble. In Your strength Lord, I can tread on lions young and old; on deadly serpents and adders.

The Lord responds:

"Because you cling to me, I will rescue you. Because you acknowledge my reputation, I will lift you high above your trouble.

"Call Me, and I will answer you. I will be with you in trouble. I will deliver you and show you honor. I will satisfy you fully with long life, and you will see My salvation."

— adapted from Psalm 91

I lift up my eyes to the hills-
from where will my help come?
My help comes from the LORD,
who made heaven and earth.
He will not let your foot be moved;
he who keeps you will not slumber.
He who keeps Israel
will neither slumber nor sleep.

The LORD is your keeper;
the LORD is your shade
at your right hand.
The sun shall not strike you by day,
nor the moon by night.

The LORD will keep you
from all evil;
he will keep your life.
The LORD will keep your going out
and your coming in
from this time on and forevermore.

— Psalm 121

Resources

For a regularly updated list of resources including those not published by Energion Publications as well as many free resources, see https://henryneufeld.com/prayer-resources.

Pathways to Prayer is a short volume that will help you get started praying and listening to God. David Moffett-Moore provides simple and effective approaches and encourages readers to move deeper in a life of prayer.

The Heart Cries Out. Another work by David Moffett-Moore, this is a devotional guide to selected Psalms. You'll find many more examples of honest prayers that you can make a part of your spiritual life.

Directed Paths. Myrtle Blabey Neufeld was a missionary nurse who found direction,

strength, and comfort in prayer. These are stories of living an active life with God.

Ultimate Allegiance: The Subversive Nature of the Lord's Prayer by Robert D. Cornwall will give new life to your study of the Lord's prayer. When the disciples wanted to learn to prayer, Jesus gave them the words of this prayer.

What can we learn about praying and also about living as disciples?

One World: The Lord's Prayer from a Process Perspective. Step back, think again, and look at the Lord's prayer with process theologian Bruce Epperly. It's hard to exhaust the meaning of the prayer that Jesus taught his disciples.

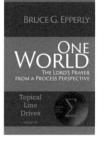

The Ground of God. Prayer isn't just an act, it's a lifestyle. This book will guide you to ways to spend more time with God and to do so more effectively. Where are you going to find God's ground?

In *I Want to Pray!* Perry Dalton, a pastor, and Henry Neufeld a teacher (and editor of this series) talk about the most basics of the basics of prayer. This booklet is in revision for its 3rd edition, but the 2nd edition is still valuable.

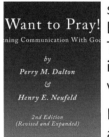

Fiction can often help us think about spiritual things, and one book that will help you with prayer is *Prayer Trilogy*, in which Kim Gordon weaves a story around God's providence. Enjoy, and be encouraged!

Prayer List

This Pamphlet Provided
Courtesy of:

Energion Publications
P. O. Box 841
Gonzalez, FL 32560

Phone: (850) 525-3916
Web: http://energion.com
E-Mail: pubs@energion.com

This booklet is available in quantity. Contact Energion Publications for more information.

ISBN: 978-1-63199-716-7
eISBN: 978-1-63199-702-0

Lightning Source UK Ltd.
Milton Keynes UK
UKRC010849200620
365294UK00002B/3

* 9 7 8 1 6 3 1 9 9 7 1 6 7 *